First published 2017
Reprinted 2019
by Subbed In

© Aisyah Shah Idil 2019

Cover design by Dan Hogan
Book design by Sam Wieck
Text set in 8pt Domaine Text

Second edition

Printed and bound in Birrarunga (Melbourne)

National Library of Australia Cataloguing-in-Publication:
Shah Idil, Aisyah
The Naming / Aisyah Shah Idil
ISBN: 9780648147503 (paperback)

Subbed In 004

All rights reserved.

This book is copyright. Apart from any fair dealing for the purposes of research, criticism, study, review or otherwise permitted under the Copyright Act, no part of this book may be reproduced by any process without permission. Inquiries should be addressed to Subbed In: hello@subbed.in

www.subbed.in

These poems were written and edited on the stolen land and waterways of the Bediagal people of the Darug nation and the Gadigal-Wangal people of the Eora nation. This book was printed and bound on the stolen lands of the Woiwurrung (Wurundjeri) and Boon Wurrung people of the Kulin nation. Sovereignty was never ceded. Aisyah Shah Idil and Subbed In pay their respects to elders, past and present.

Always was, always will be Aboriginal land.

'And He taught Adam the names of all things.'
(2:30)

I dreamt of a white tiger tonight. It prowled underneath the floorboards, played checkers with my son.

Unclaimed spirits are dangerous.

But this one – this one feels like home.

Ahmad, are you telling your adik nonsense jinn stories again?

(Aiyoh, tak tahu. Mak balik, pukul kamu!)

It's not nonsense to me, Mak.

Abang told me them. And before that, Pak Nga. And before him, Nenek. It's passed on to me. I can't escape it.

Yellow

Yorleny tells me
that her mother, Vicky,
loves my scarf.

That in-between her chattering Spanish
¿Tu hambre?
¡Mucho polvo!

Is a secret desire for the yellow fabric
draped around my face.
Yorleny laughs at this. She asks her mother

Where on earth she would wear it
in this sleepy mountain town of
Ciudad Colón.

But it is too late. Already, the scarf is hers.
Inside, I see myself
tear it hastily off my head and

Press it tenderly
to her hands.
To be tied around her handbag,

Draped along her shoulders.
Pinned softly,
giggling,

Around her warm face –
To become a sunflower stamp.
A marigold in bloom.

Where were you on 9/11?

I SAID I LOVED YOU AND I WANTED WAR TO STOP
I SAID I LOVED YOU AND I WANTED MY FATHER HERE
I SAID I LOVED YOU AND I WANTED I WANTED
OLIVE TREES IN GROVES FULL I WANTED
JUSTICE UNDER MY PALMS

NOBODY ROLL OUT THE TANKS NOBODY ROLL
OUT THE ROCKETS
I SAID I LOVED YOU AND I WANTED MEN
WOMEN
BOYS GIRLS
SAFE

LISTEN
THIS LONGING IS TOO BIG TO FIT ON A MAP

THIS LONGING IS TOO PRECIOUS TO FIT ON A MAP
THIS
LONGING IS TOO OLD TO FIT ON A MAP

AFFIRM LIFE
AFFIRM LIFE
AFFIRM
LIFE

Water

I let
the water
seep over
me.

I let
it climb
my shoulders,
my collar
bones, my
neck.

The smooth
slope of
my lobes

The ske
letal swirl
of my
ear.

I let
it slide
inside.

Until I was fat with it.
Until I was full.

Until the worldly pings
and screams
and worries
and lusts-

Went.

I have no desire to die.
Oblivion is not appealing to me.

Leaving this body is-
Leaving, not being left.

Being a blade of grass, a solid oak.
A cat that knows only how to be a cat.

I have been struggling, Lord,
with my hijab.

Hijaaaaaaaaaaaaaaaaaaahb.

I will not be
dead and buried
in pants, skirts,
vests or sunglasses.

The Indignity! The Shame!

Death shrouds are less intimidating
when I realise
I have been wearing
part of one my entire life.

Will it be a ship
carrying me across the earthly plains?
The only covering I have of earth and heaven?

Do not uncover my hair when I am dead.
Wrap me up in muslin and pandan leaves.
Oil my skin until I stain the earth.

Reminder

Lines drawn separate skin from flesh, trees from groves. We were born together on the open road of the jacaranda tree, neither twins nor brothers, but two lovers who approached each other shyly and with some reluctance.

A believer is like a date palm tree – all goodness. Yet you choked on your mother's milk so much that none of those sitting underneath the shade of migration thought you would live. They thought my flat nose an omen of misfortune or ill health; rubbing softened dates on your gums, praying in your fleshy ears.

But March, which has the power to bring wealth flush from dry topsoil, turned us well. You know this only to remember that life did not come to you easily, but obstinately, like a young cat who does not recognise your scent.

So remind me as I remind you. Of love, kindness and justice perfectly placed. Hope is difficult to barter, but try anyway. They will tell you that you are mistaken, but do not listen. Hold out your memories in your palms without shame. They are all we have and they matter.

Arrange the keys from most-used to disused and make sure the doorknobs are oiled well. They creak from pride and a stubbornness to ask: have we been forgotten? Have you given up on us, have you given us what we deserve? I told them that I had never heard anything so wretched in my life and they laughed, mocking: have you lived at all?

So carry me, and do not fret if the threshold follows us. She too, wonders if she has a place here.

The Essay

---

[1] Here, summertime means less rain than normal. Means the fans whir a little more wheezily, that the blankets turn into mattress covers and that weddings under the block end before 2pm. That's what she's been told, at least. She's made sure to stock up on tidbits of knowledge. It makes answering strangers' questions a little more bearable.

[2] 'With white people,' my mother says, 'simple. Just ask their names and tell jokes. Or else they get nervous too easily.'

[3] Most likely an allusion to the *pontianak*, a Malay jinn.

"...spirit of women who died while pregnant. Usually dressed in white with long, black hair..." (ibid., pg. 543)

[1] 'Because of the finality of this kind of travel, one must pack lightly – and with great thought. The majority of clothing is replaceable, but good-quality outerwear, sturdy shoes and clean underwear make this undertaking far less arduous. Take care to comfort your child while on the passage. He or she can sense your tension, and the balm of a young smile can provide more relief than the most committed attendant.' (Ahmad 1951, pg. 75)

[2] Joyce, J. *and yes I said yes I will Yes*.
Plath, S. *I am I am I am*.

[3] To the woman who imitated my mother's accent, I say:
can you? Can you get that inflection of humor in your t's /

Can you coax the grief out and
feel it tremble / Can you wean
softness out and hold it open /

Her words are weighty for those who don't know how to carry them, and so can you?

[4] This photograph was never found.

---

[1] At Block 816, lizards crawl in
through the cracks. They leave
coffee stains on the table,
tap tiny claws
on empty
plates. Tear
open our letters.

[2] Mispronounce our names.

Laylatul-Qadr

My nephew is born
on the 27th night of
Ramadan.
When I peek out the window in the morning
I see that it has rained overnight.

*

His name is Mikail
like the angel that lights up the sky.

In Hebrew, this means
What is like God?

When I hold him
I begin to cry.

His mother, exhausted and
attached to a catheter

rests against the bed and
remembers the harrowing night.

I am awed by the pain her tiny hips
vibrate with

on a night better than a thousand months.

*

Nabra Hassanen. Ricky John Best.
Taliesin Myrrdin Namkai-Meche.
Makram Ali. Tehran. Grenfell Tower.
The silent, the mourning,
the countless dead this holy month.

Afterwards, the roads
are unbelievably full. People pour into the
sidewalk, pen their messages of hope,
and send their grief to each other

As if all night they had dreamed about
what they would like their lives to be
and imagined only closeness.

Malay Sketches

Jawi

Malay

        kepala ▊▊▊ nasi,
          ke atas bamboo alas
tangan macam-macam kepala burung ▊▊
    sambal pedas, ▊

▊▊▊ kari ▊▊▊
basuh pingan, kamu tidak buat
▊▊▊
kursi macam ▊
Tidak orang nak basuh pingan.

Kita semua ▊▊ anak-anak,
  anak-anak, ▊ dan ▊ dan
    di atas ▊▊ di dalam ▊ bilik tidur,
kita ▊▊▊

Atas ▊▊▊ cermain atas
▊▊, Mak saya ▊ :
Kita semua cinta Isa sama-sama.

▊▊▊-merah ▊▊ .
Dia tauh apa kita tak -
▊▊▊

Dengan ▊ macam ▊ kita ▊ air ▊,
▊ , ▊ ,
▊▊ rukuh,
▊ tidur. ▊ solat ▊,
tapi kita tak ▊ .
Allah dah nampak kita ▊ .

English

Bobbing heads circle platters of rice,
tender knees sinking into bamboo mats
hands like sparrow heads press
into spicy chilli paste, tingling.

Fingers covered in curry point to the sink -
wash the plates, you didn't do it last time.
Backs slouch against scratched leather
couches like restless puddles.
No one wants to wash the plates.

We are fishermen's children, rubber-tapper's
children, all skin and lips and easy bruises. Lying
on pockmarked floors in shared bedrooms,
we sneeze from dust crowding old wedding photos.

At the top of a smudged mirror
is a bumper sticker
filled with air bubbles:

We Love Jesus Too.
Weathered palm heels that smooth over
red block letters ignore our scoffs.
She knows what we don't:
even dappled light blinds some.

With arms like reed sticks we stalk water
droplets, drag them from wrist to elbow,
ankle to toe, stretch in that bow, press
the forehead down in sleep. Quiet prayer
leads to thoughts like soft dough,
but we don't worry.

We figure God has seen us in less.

Instances of Allahu Akbar

My mother, after
a long period of somnolence,
where getting up is only possible
through divine assistance.

The hasty search for a
mobile phone, adhan blaring
in a full train carriage,
a work meeting, an elevator.

Tugging on the wispy beard
of a humiliated friend.

A moment of bravado
at the circus of security.
Shushed in LAX by my
terrified husband.

A yelp of ecstasy. The shirtless
circuit. An animated Messi scores
three goals in five minutes.

Voice soft, autumnal.
Fingers still wet from crushed date.
A newborn sleeps.

So you want to be an artist

ARTIST

The serif pokes your tongue.

What an excellent idea, lauds your white guidance counsellor. Her hair is bright pink and she houses small birds in her chest. Your claws shake with hunger as you reach for them. Maybe this is the magic she eats for dinner. Maybe they gift her small jewels she uses to pay for her mother's medical bills. Maybe this actually is possible.

You huddle in front of your blue screen. Every line you write brings etches of sharp fingernails across hair, skin and lips. Little cockroaches nibble on your toes and you carefully carry them to your kitchen sink. Stay there. I'm c r e a t i n g.

Tomorrow, your thick lashes spit on you. They dribble down the sides of your face and into the cavernous echoes of your clavicle's quiver. Gluggy fear churns across your chest and pulls your bolder shoulders down to melt like soggy ice-cream. A two is emblazoned across your forehead.

What a cruel number to give someone at a poetry slam. A zero would be kinder.

Your masseuse asks you if her hands are too hard. You moan noisily and she recoils from you. She sees intimately the birthmark across your left thigh and wishes your self-care back to journaling and prayer. Back to singing in showers and throwing eggs at trees. Far away from her and the flakes of dry skin you've left on her hands.

A spotlight appears above the both of you and she clicks her oily fingers like a jazz singer. Slinky in batik. Stinky in egg sauce. You affirm the valuable work she does and enjoy the show.

A bus woofs past. An oil canister bursts on the sidewalk. Your brother calls you stupid.

Logic demands you pay the bills. 'It's two weeks late, babe.' She leans on the doorway of your Punchbowl apartment. Fish swim through her dreads and brush away the frizz. 'You got a book for me?'

You grandly present it to her. It's your first one: about an office worker that does everything but his office work. She flicks to the last page and sees it was all a dream. A whistle flies through her teeth. 'Original! Never read this before.' Your poetry disappears inside her bag. 'I'll come back for the next one in a month.'

A big smile languishes around your teeth. It notices that you floss every day and tells you. You politely excuse yourself to keep writing. You are a serious artist and tell her so. She stubbornly refuses to leave and resigned, you carry her into your bedroom. Here, she tells you, she'll stay.

Flagbearer

i will be your woman/bearer

wombs moulded by

the pomegranate heads of babies
with sharp teeth
who tear our lips open and speak
drive-by hate, morning-news-lies.

i will hold the silky butterfly
in my palms, flag high, I'll feel it   billow

they have brought war to our
breakfasts, feed my women
morsels of tar

coat my men
in blue-black blossoms

spy our   flags

let me remind you
our Beloved is closer to you
than the vein

don't be precious, now
bullets down our thighs

our steel warms wet   night

Pontianak

My grandmother
flees, staring down
at the deep sunken and skeletal.
Her belly is huge

Her husband, silent.
They have no medals on
this side of the war, but
they do have stories

Slowly

their leaky boat tears open the sea

Today, an old anxiety
fuzzes inside me
and so –
Bring out the drums! Bring
out the dance!

I pound the bed, I
do my vocal scales. I do
not need the small and
needy bleat

of understanding. Maybe I
am sad because my grandmother was,
because her grandmother was, because
over and over again,

we waste time wanting
different lives.

I stamp
my feet on the floorboards,
and breathe in small, sharp
exhalations.

Soon,
we will gather and mutter
about pontianaks and magic.
Maybe they exist, maybe not.
But the grief of women

Losing children is an old
and timeless tale. Cloak it
in myth or candlelight if you want.
But keep telling them

Because then no-one is surprised
that when the white moon rises,
some of them lash out with a cold
and screeching edge.

# Dear Abu Ghraib,

A friend's letter is lost and the postcard needs an address. Neither of these reach the end intended but they reach one regardless. The pen has been lifted and all that is left is to trace the dry ink.

I'll meet you, finally, at the threshold of torture reports and the second half of my childhood. You've missed out on so much, I want to tell you. The humidity never leaves you lonely. The television screens never leave you lonely. The birds fly into our houses here and spread their wings in our closets. They are lost and we want to keep them that way.

You kiss me on my nose and say: in this myth you have created of me, I was never lonely.

The salty seawater fruits spilled over and you were never left hungry.

This is your autumn from an endless summer, a city's fatigue from an endless war.

The doctor purses his lips. Has he taken his vitamins? No, but he remembers things no-one his age should. Has he spoken to you lately? He wants to smile, but his mouth only speaks in loss and lack. Has he remembered the names of his fathers? He is still young and his fathers do not look at him.

Paradisial

A DAY SO FINE
THE AIR IS WARM, THE GRASS SOFT
CATS STRETCH OUT BESIDE ME IN THE MORNING SUN

THERE IS NOTHING ON EARTH I WANT TO POSSESS
NO PERSON WORTH MY ENVYING

TO THINK I AM MYSELF INVITES NO EMBARRASSMENT
NOR SHAME
ANY HURT I HAVE SUFFERED, I FORGOT

WHEN I LOOK UP, I SEE THE BLUE SKY AND CLOUDS

The Usual

quiet, laughing,
you've got
an eyelash.
> *right. there.*

cold tea dregs float
like drowned ants

        dust crowns the bald heads
        of books, too long

                toenails knock
                sneakers' guts

my sour-breathed sweet
someone's sun pressed
desperately against the
window

hardened blu-tac, fallen
birthday banners.

        mislabeled
        pill boxes.

slivered almond moon
crumbs scattered
armpits, hair, fingertips.
tiny you-were-here's

skies west of the sea, milk-soaked
later it will rain, earth shifting
floorplans in righteous fury.

i'll empty the compost tubs
the ground's forehead kissed
damp with wet leaves

i love you/i miss you/i put the bins out.

AUTHOR ACKNOWLEDGEMENTS

To my poetry mentors, Raidah, Caits and Ni'mah, for their critical eyes and advice;

To my publishers, Stacey, Dan and Rory, for their faith in me and this book;

To my parents, Mak and Abah, for the ripening fruits of their sacrifice;

To my spiritual teachers, for reminding me of the most Beloved;

To my husband, Adam, for continually lowering his gaze from my flaws;

To my friends and companions, whose hearts, homes and prayers have perfumed my life;

To God, Most High.

Thank you. From what well of mercy did this sweet fragrance come from?

With so much gratitude,
Aisyah

ABOUT THE AUTHOR

Aisyah Shah Idil is an Australian writer and poet. Her work has been featured in the Islamic Museum of Australia, *Language on the Move*, *Love Haqtually*, the *Sydney Morning Herald* and the *Digging Deep Facing Self International* anthology. *The Naming* is her first book.

'Malay Sketches' was originally published in *Language on the Move* (2015).

Subbed In is a not-for-profit DIY literary organisation and small press based in Sydney, Australia. Subbed In's program of publications and events aim to elevate the voices of trans people, people of colour, non-binary people, sex workers, women, people with a disability, LGBTQIA+ people, First Nations people, survivors, working class people, and anyone who finds themselves on the margins of the supremely white, cis, heteronormative, capitalist, colonial, ableist, patriarchal hellscape in which we live.

For more information visit: *www.subbed.in*

ALSO AVAILABLE FROM SUBBED IN

When I die slingshot my ashes onto the surface of the moon
by Jennifer Nguyen

HAUNT (THE KOOLIE)
by Jason Gray

The Hostage
by Šime Knežević

blur by the
by Cham Zhi Yi

wheeze
by Marcus Whale

If you're sexy and you know it slap your hams
by Eloise Grills

Parenthetical Bodies
by Allison Gallagher

Girls and Buoyant
by Emily Crocker

www.ingramcontent.com/pod-product-compliance
Lightning Source LLC
Chambersburg PA
CBHW030530010526
44110CB00048B/1060